I0798597

Without Benefit of Words

Without Benefit of Words

Kathleen Wall

Turnstone Press

Turnstone Press
607-100 Arthur Street
Winnipeg, Manitoba
Canada R3B 1H3

Turnstone Press gratefully acknowledges the assistance of the Canada Council, the Manitoba Arts Council and the Saskatchewan Arts Board in the publication of this book.

Saskatchewan Arts Board

Cover design and illustration: Roger Lusty

This book was printed and bound in Canada by Hignell Printing Limited for Turnstone Press.

Some of these poems have appeared in *Antigonish Review*, *Blue Buildings*, *Contemporary Verse 2*, *The Fiddlehead*, *minnesota review* and *Queen's Quarterly*.

Canadian Cataloguing in Publication Data

Wall, Kathleen, 1950-
Without benefit of words

Poems.
ISBN 0-88801-161-X

I. Title.

PS8595.A55W48 1991 C811/.54 C91-097161-7
PR9199.3.W255W48 1991

Acknowledgements

I would like to thank John McElheny, Tom McIntyre and Robert Haugh for their early encouragement of my writing. In times of the most potent disbelief in my craft and voice, I remember their words of reassurance and support.

I must also thank the Manitoba Writers' Guild for support they gave in various ways. Kate Bitney, who arranged poetry readings, helped me to end a writer's block. The Guild's Mentor Program allowed me to have an invaluable apprenticeship with Patrick Friesen. And of course, Patrick deserves many thanks for his willingness to read my work and to comment on it with great humanism and a wonderful sense of craft, as well as for his readiness to discuss anything from philosophy to poetics. Since I tend to be something of a recluse as a writer, I have valued the Guild's encouragement. A final thanks to my editor at Turnstone, Dan Lenoski. He was uncanny about rooting out wordiness and verbosity, especially in the early poems, and his suggestions helped to make this volume, which has been accumulating over a long period of time, more poetically coherent.

As necessary as the gift of direct encouragement is the gift of absolute faith. For their unconditional belief in me, I must thank my parents, Lawrence and Doris Wall, and my daughter, Veronica.

Many people contributed to the de-griefing that shaped "Metaphysics of Divorce": Joanne, Elizabeth, Bernard, Marnie, Beth, Diane, Stan, Ivy, Niagara, Bugs—and perhaps Veronica most of all. I thank them all for returning me to the world of pleasure and joy.

"Metaphysics of Divorce" is a purely interior account of my experience of divorce. Being entirely subjective (as we are during such grief), it in no way is meant to reflect actual events or make judgements of others' intentions.

This book is for John McElheny
and
of course
for Veronica

Contents

Dumb Animals

Icarus

The smell of green walls and dew
lay in the morning beside the brood
of plucked birds.
Father at his tidy fire
moulded wings and smiled.

I smelled the death of birds,
the soft wax of sanctuaries,
and snow: something cold
from another season
that hinted at storms and corners.

Father, craftsman, unconcerned,
worked with the slowness
of perfection and just as slowly told
how the minotaur slept for a day or two
after each feast. We were safe, he said,

except from our own foolishness,
and smiled with eyes that would not see
that labyrinthine paths are blind,
that he himself has forged dead ends
for youths and birds.

He never taught me to fly—
having nothing but warnings
and delight in his own cleverness,
his ache to go seaward and escape
his own devices. Not wanting height

but distance. While I flew
ignoring every sign: the glide
of wax down my back,
the smell of burnt feathers,
my father's cries, the bright new heat.

For what seduced all sense
was the sight below,
unbroken by labyrinthine walls,
entire: gardens, beast, the unflying bones.
And my reflection in the water.

Humansong: Words/Music

I Words

Like a clairvoyant
I hear words out of context
that wind foggy through my head unsought:

  If you can't own it,
  Screw it/ or kill it.

The weapons for these sentiments
are intimate household items
  butcher knife,
  insecticide,
  nakedness,
  fishbowls and divorce papers,
  hand, fist,
  mouths—oh, yes, mouths, words.

Who walks to the microphone in my inner ear
and seeks the airing of grievances?
They sing the humansong of anger and possession,
the song of the owners,
verses about trees and meat and women.
Then it echoes in an anxious key
in hope I will hear something
under the whisper of obedience.

II Music

Their voices come like lines in a glass fugue:
the subject repeated at endless intervals in the dominant
answered in frightened minor.
Humansong.
Behind its strident discords
in the rests between subject and answer
I hear the counterpoint of sea, trees, creatures
in keys of fur and green and earth.

Humansong. Is this the melody we pass from year to year,
place to place,
encapsulating our history and our present:
        If you can't own it,
        Screw it/ or kill it.
Is this the humansong that echoes
up and down the coasts of earth and love?

Death Songs for My Daughter

1. Murder

Every night I sing five lullabies
and hold my daughter till
she blindly seeks her bed
and the friendly
clutch of creatures
we arrange
in their own places   night
after night.

This is my charm
against nightmares   the only
armour, guidebook, rations
for her night journey.
This is our pact
in the darker love of night.

* * *

One night last week,
the same hour
when I sang my child to sleep,
her aunt was murdered.
No charmed songs, no
familiar helping creature
protected her,
she had no armour
against a man with a screwdriver
who left her moaning
behind a car wash.
"I needed to kill someone"
he said.

* * *

Now every night I lie.
The songs, the bears
are pretence of safe nights.

My charms will fail. I cannot
always sing songs that do not keen
the night as it is.

2. Growth

On a nursery-school field trip
to the Faculty of Animal Science she saw

"A tiny horse swimming in a bottle,
Mama,
and a pig with two heads—
he was swimming too
in a jar
in lots of jars on big
black tables all
the animals were swimming"

in formaldehyde.
Delighted
with the little swimming
creatures, the two-headed grim beasts
she chattered for a week
about swimming in big jars
on black tables.

* * *

Scarcely a year later
the Ugly Duckling floats toward a swan,
knowing that radiant grace
marks mercy.
His deformity is a grief
that her child's beauty should not know.
Yet his wish for death
too real
shocks her to tears.
The Velveteen Rabbit
narrowly escapes
a funeral pyre, and no
explanations
happy endings
reassure her into reading
that book again. She demands
to know the end of a book before
she commits herself to the beginning.

Something died
in her that year
something with a bright shape
and no shadows.
And something—
some two-headed beast—
was born.

Cosmogony

For Diane Whitehouse,
her paintings of *Rooms and Journeys*

I

These paintings of Rooms
are cosmogonies: you have built
spaces no one has seen:
Corners with no cosiness,
meetings of mind-walls
the colour of thoughts
that go blank upon themselves
into large spaces of quiet shock,
corners with pewter mirrors
that reflect
nothing,
trees that will never grow
except as umbrellas of thought,
creatures to which you wish
to say goodbye
but greet in paint
in an exorcism of acceptance.

II

I think of a painting by Munch
in his northern greys:
Two hungry souls sit at table.
There,
just out of reach,
is a bottle of wine—perhaps
some fruit, bread, cheese
that they cannot bend to touch
in their greydim stiffness.
That hunger creates
a feast of famine in their eyes
a cosmos of want that reaches
over the distance of ochre emptiness
across the table, out of the painting.

III

There is a cosmogony
for hotel rooms.
Take
        the pictures
        of barns and stags and sunsets
        off the putty-coloured walls;
Strip
        down to bare
        lack of place;

this room becomes a canvas
for imaginations' needs.
From the bed
the window is an open abstract
sky, a few wires, rooftops.

Cosmos of lovers or loneliness:
Lovers holographed from memory
brushed into being on bare walls,
shaped and shadowed in the putty-
coloured paint. Impressions
of wine-lonely days
or coffee-stark nights
glimmer in the dappled bureau mirror,
impressions live as wet paint,
or dull as scratched hotel glasses.

In the bare ceiling
or its crackled reflection
in the mirror
there is no comfort: compose
impose
your own vision
on the putty walls.

IV

Across the tables
in the dark of Holiday Inn bars
paunched businessmen get up
passion
for their putty-faced wives.

In this dark I have seen men
imagine into being
        sylphs
                whose eyelids shimmer blue-green
        courtesans
                whose mouths pulse red speech
from the dreary of wives they have not loved
for twenty years.

There is a contract of pretence
made across those tables
by women desperate enough to agree
to behave like girls
and men horny for legitimate sex
—a contract of bright laughter and innuendo.

That hunger creates
a feast of famine in their eyes
a cosmos of want that reaches
over the distance of emptiness
across the table
in a darkened bar.

Swan Lake

1.

Passion:

I first knew it   as   grace
innocent as girls in mauve sashes
at barre
formalized as pirouettes and pas de deux
costumed in blue velvet, silver braid, white tulle.

Steady, serious Prince
and swan-shy girl
danced their formal desire
deep in chastity's cool blue wood
as if the darkness of the sorcerer's spells
    were not their darkness
as if unfaithfulness
    were only evil magic
as if the nighttime chastity of swans
    were deadly.

An aesthete's idea of love
is a dance
pure, taut, above
all controlled.
A dance made
not of bodies but of lines
grace   tulle   velvet. The dark
mirror/minor side of love
breaking only
in the music.

2.

As a young girl
seeing Swan Lake
denatured desire
poured it into a curved, antique vessel
that I clasped
to my breast
with balletic drama
and sipped
during porcelain daydreams.

I superimposed blue forests
on red Fords
and the merest sibilant thought
of what I had not done   but
might   have wanted
brought uneven pulse to unremembered places.
Chaste kisses fluttered through those years.
Lips with no more passion
than swansfeathers
brushed other lips, cheeks, eyes.

This dance of swans
and the stiff shuffle of adolescents
moving to the rhythmic cough of chaperones
collided with the stealthy guilt of hotels
with my love coming to me in jockey shorts
and bare, hairy legs.
Romance is something you look at
think about;
but neither looking
nor thinking
I watched swan's white rush
swept out of the window
into the river.

3.

The ballet's cyclorama
moonlit wood and clear blue lake
stretched taut between
dreams of romance
and the undreaming loss of virginity.
And off stage
I stood poised to see both
pure blue wood
and hotel room. That the fabric
did not shred and expose the back room world
was more shock
than the unthinking, unhalting pull
of sex.

Seeing Swan Lake again
fifteen years later
discloses naïveté's source.
I drink again of denatured desire
and taste now the bitter undertone of shame.
Passion
is not a ballet choreographed
a century ago
but a dance that   springs
and bursts
through blue forests and white tulle
to bloom red and joyful.

Batterie de cuisine

Cleaning chickens for dinner,
looking at the imperturbable
suburban houses,
thinking of my mother who deftly
exorcised pinfeathers from A&P fryers,
I finally pull out the bagged guts,
rinse out the bits of heart left behind
by a careless butcher.
All this death quivers in my hand.
That lawn across the street
with its stucco house and flowers
doesn't know the death
that inhabits chicken guts
or the death of what can go on
inside its own kitchen, as when my mother,
cleaning chickens,
told me she never wanted to get pregnant,
never wanted another child in her guts,
never attached that child to her heart.
Now I am cleaning chickens,
pulling out the bits of heart
left behind by a careless butcher,
the death of my own heart
quivering in my hand.

Bill of Fare

The magazine rack at Kent's Cafe
has a menu of free
philosophies: *Plain Truth* and *Luck*
come with the daily special.

Plain Truth proclaims
famine in Ethiopia:
Its cover waves
in the air-conditioned breeze,
banner for their crusade
and our salvation,
its device the limbs and bellies
of children sated with hunger:

> Give—
> buy your tickets
> for the celestial lottery.
> God knows
> what heavenly prizes there are
> for your abstract love
> and concrete money.

Poetic justice would demand
a price for our indifference:
an eternal drought spent holding
a starving child. But *Plain Truth*
has forgotten poetic justice.

Luck stands, pot-bellied,
with his dowdy delighted wife
and his jackpot.
He is a promise of prosperity for the deserving
buyers of lottery tickets, of luck everlasting.
He knows there is some justice to his win,
some deed, once done, important, forgotten,
that defeats the odds for him.
But his cover photo is made
from the melded negatives of those
for whom there is no lottery, no tickets,
no loose change to gamble.

Aside from these tracts, the Cafe
offers no other magazines, no news
of *True Love* or *Time*. At the stand
one pays for the comfort of soup and sweets
or chooses tickets for the 649,
paying the fat proprietor
as he sings to himself.

Dumb Animals: 1

On Breaking My Gentlest Cat's Jaw

An awkward parcel,
a cat's greeting on the stair.

I trip, parcel falls, cat flees
under the bed, bloody with broken jaw.

By the time I coax her out she smells
—for the first time I remember—
purely animal, the meaty smell of blood and fear,
while I am the logic of emergencies.

Now, while she sleeps, mending,
I lay our incomprehensions
side by side,
to smooth them out,
these two pieces of crumpled paper,
difficult to read.

I ask the human questions of cause and conscience,
enquire of the physics of accidents:
how two inches of a box catching the stair's edge,
a door that catches ten seconds too soon
could break the gentlest creature
who blesses my household
with her meditations upon purr,
who knows the sound of pages turning in a book
means lap.

She wonders about longing that becomes greeting,
about the shock of heavy hurt,
the smell of blood,
ancient to a domestic cat.
She knows the kithless, severed silence
of feline pain,
the still withdrawal from the pleasures
that muddy
our earthly expectations,
the moment's focus that accepts
a broken jaw not as fate but as the present.
She makes no lists of points
where accident became pain,
where my clumsiness might have been stopped
by a heartier lunch, warmer weather, help with the parcel.

Her silence stuns me
with its shapely grounding in the present,
its lyrical lack of reproach.

Silence seems to make possible
her purring two days later
as she calmly lets the other cats,
hostile to her foreign, broken smell,
nuzzle her fur
while she heals
in my lap.

Dumb Animals: 2

My cat sits frozen in tired vigilance,
head bowed, her green eyes fixed
as if they cast to hell to study pain. For days
she does not bathe herself, but moves

with concentrating slowness
to her hellish vantage points
around the house. But never
more than three days.

I know the hollows where she stares.
I walk round them—as if they were
places I could avoid—until vision
becomes voice

and I ride talk's mineshaft
into caverns with dripping walls
and demented fuses that whisper
their way to explosions.

Take language from me. Joy
can beat in flight or beam in eyes
glaze bright fur and ripple muscle.
But pain needs words or wounds.

Dumb Animals: 3

Sparrows, flitting and chirping
in a fir-dark tree,
do not seem to tell one another
they will die of the cold if this weather lasts

another week. They ruffle their feathers
to the buffeting wind, and all of February
come daily to the feeder, looking fat
and satisfied, sounding perfectly cheery.

But humans in down and fur grow bitter,
rage at cold-dark days, make threats
they cannot keep, shaking voices like fists
at cold indifference.

If voice were a chirp or a croon
could song rage at winter
or must it hope of spring?

Dumb Animals: 4

"There is no prediscursive reality."
—Jacques Lacan

Two black cats meet at bedtime
to put me to sleep.
One tilts her nose to the ceiling,
the second echoes the gesture
in silhouette against the grey wall.
What have they said to one another:
is this tilt of the head a greeting,
an agreement, a truce, a diagnosis?

As they settle me down for sleep
I wonder how much discourse goes on in my house
without benefit of words.
Do wintering spiders in the corners of my living room
wave a semaphore of fruit flies
multiplied by faceted eyes?
The sparrows nesting in my kitchen vents
are very quiet:
soon the bug-anxious peeping of fledglings
that starts soft as a cat's snore
will drive me nearly crazy.
But what do they say now,
so quiet it does not filter down the plastic hose
and sing to me as I cook? Is there a language
of feather flicking meant to fool
and comfort
anxious homeowners and discourse analysts
with fluttered silence?

Without words you nearly outwit Lacan
who stills reality with his claim to language.
My cats unfreeze joy's indeterminacy
with wordless purr of pleased longing
qualified by infinite inflection of tail.
Blue height is thought with wings,
seed with the downward whip of tail feathers.
The paradox of death and meal
is mediated only by web and enzyme,
poison bite and quick shake of head.
And what discourse ever explains
hungry waiting,
makes it more or less real?

Careful, Lacan,
lest you claim more than you want
and annihilate the prediscursive silences
after the moments of love,
before death.

Yes: and I use words.

The Legion Gardens

for Susan Bukta and her father

These houses—nothing about them makes sense.
Nice wooden lawnchairs, painted white each year,
on porches facing railroad tracks.
The picture windows rattle crazy threats
when trains go by.
Gardens they call this place,
but there's only the odd birch and small blue spruce.
Sam has flowers,
but he grows them in half a wine barrel
he brought back from someplace west
he went last year. He's planted
purple petunias, says it makes a grand ashtray.

But the houses—no basements to them.
I suppose they didn't expect us to have much
to store—a few scrapbooks and service albums
in junk and memories.
Furnishings are regulation—
yellowed venetian blinds
that bar the sun or stripe my cigarette smoke
at sunrise,
the nubbly sofa and chair that match.
Twin beds—no more twinning
they expect of us.
They're more like motel rooms, really,
the kind that come with furnished kitchenettes
that I took in some small town each summer
near the hunting but not too far from the bars
and cheap enough.

These houses—plunked down next to the tracks
in a neighbourhood full of kids—
17-year-olds with families of their own half-started
women whose men don't want them
or their bastards.
We are walled in by the sound of trains
and the curses of disappointment that ring
from the corner store.

So we talk to each other.
Sam makes good coffee, and he's always generous
with his cigarettes—hands me one over the deal table
with his waxy yellow fingers and always tries to tell me
that's one less coffin nail for him.
We make the houses yellow
with cigarette smoke and the old fear we breathe
but will not talk about.
Sam, here, he has bad dreams.
I can hear him across the garden
on summer nights when there are no trains.

I don't have nightmares.
My sleep is like these houses—
yellow smoky regulation sleep
and regulation dreams.
I don't expect them to change
before I die.

There is a man I envy, one I watch
in smoky dawns.
He walks along the track to throw the switches,
leaning his weight in, thrusting out,
taking his cigarette from his mouth and moving on
to the next switch. There is a beauty
in the way he throws himself into change,
strides out of sight along a track
that goes

everywhere.

Descent of Inanna

Of Ereshkigal

I have come to Ereshkigal's realm
not in open choice but from need
of her dark place for nakedness—
so heavy were my clothes.

The sunlight scorched the skin
of my bare wrist when,
for relief, I moved the heavy cuff of my robe
as I examined dry fields.

When I swung my foot in the lukewarm river
to thank the reluctant flood
the hem of my gown was weighted
by silt and water.

I dared not remove the robes of state
and lose my place of power and dignity
in the upper world of light. I would cease
to be seen Inanna, Queen of Heaven:

Better some sacrifice
to ennoble my tired nakedness—
so I thought: to join Ereshkigal
in mourning for her mate Gugalanna.

After all, one goes to her world primarily
to mourn
oneself, one's life, other smaller, larger deaths
that crystallize along our cavern walls
in wounds or diamonds.

Such deaths are always attended
by indignity;
even in Ereshkigal's dark,
invisible, secret indignities of loss or wound or absence
glow like unhealthy conspirators
irradiated, green.

* * *

Bordering her purple realm
are seven gates.
At each she demands a sacrifice
a casting off of clothes and roles.

Casual ceremony is implied by the tired gatekeeper
who took my robe,
the state seal deep in the pocket,
hung it on a golden hook
and gave me a head of wheat in return.
I might have been checking my coat at an inn.

At the first three gates, the same casual exchange,
this lifting of ceremonial weight,
the head of wheat in return.
The deep silent rest of my shoulders
and my eyes. We cannot see in Ereshkigal's netherworld
and peacefully give in to sleepy blindness.

But at the fourth gate some warning—
an acid smell that penetrates like venom
toward the top of the skull.
I breathed only shallowly, and as the keeper
took the last of my clothes—
leaving ring, amulet, crown—
I felt the vacuum of nakedness
empty my breast of feeling.

At each successive gate he took
some part of self with the decorative touches
that indicated my estate:
with ring went feeling hands,
the amulet worn on my arm took with it
the ability to hold,
with crown went thought
until I was truly naked, truly dead, meat
before Ereshkigal. She casts her eyes
on what I cannot transcend,
and I see what nakedness means:
not freedom from heavy robes
but that my own eyes cannot condemn me less
than the dead eyes of Ereshkigal.

And how has Ereshkigal arranged this:
that I hang as meat on her corpse hooks
yet watch the flies eagerly examine
meat as both food and as place to lay eggs.
I am the flies that examine
the scar from falling when I was eight,
the greying hair of a crone.
Walking over my face I see
reflected in my corpse's eyes
my thousand eyes.

Journal: Wednesday, December 3, 1986

There are strange moments of lucidity: after a wave of the unnameable despair has crested—a wave one wishes to drown in—one is suddenly aware of the cat on one's lap, the precise texture of fur, the way she moulds her pleasure to my hand. One is drowned in a sense of purposelessness, then maps one's next day carefully, trying to plan for the sense of accomplishment that allows one to say 'I'm sane; I'm functioning.'—But trying also to make only slight, reasonable demands. I found my mind, like that of someone trying to plan the perfect murder, plotting my death so it would not hurt my child—and realizing at the same moment the insanity of the idea 'to die and not hurt my child.' It is unthinkable; I thought it nevertheless.

Of Ninshubur, my assistant

Even while my eyes stare
at the corpse I am,
at the corpse where I lay my eggs,
I see Ninshubur
who watches the flood I have summoned
and knows its progress.
Ninshubur
who studies Nanna of the moon
and reads his power to draw the seed.
She arranges for me the return of the fertile earth
even while she mourns.
Ninshubur's gift is to beat the dirge drum while she plants,
to sing in two keys: lament and praise.
Efficient Ninshubur who sends water and sprouted grain
to redeem me from Ereshkigal.

She teaches Enki's two small clay mourners
a dirge for Inanna and drought and unsprouted seed
and the song of earth about to bloom, of Inanna's return,
to admit Ereshkigal's grief and seduce it from her.

Hearing the two songs, rich, twined,
we both relent:
I give up the need for nakedness that brought me here,
stop staring at the corpse I oddly willed,
Ereshkigal lifts me off the peg of her disdain.
I walk naked to the final gate and redeem,
with my seven heads of wheat,
my clothes, my state, and a handful of sprouts from
  Ninshubur.

The light is strangely green,
like morning filtered through water and trees. I hum
the song I learned from the clay mourner, not the lament,
but the bloom, busy myself with clothing,
arrange my robes: I like the purple weight around my feet,
lean my leg into silk,
emerge from the netherworld entryway
a woman with a few nightmares to puzzle out.

Journals of an Urban Gardener

Supernova
March 31

Set in water, on a late afternoon
the green-tight buds of daffodils
begin
to loosen,
their cool green light peels
from trumpet to petals.
Overnight they ripen; gold flows
to the six points like molten heat
stored in stars,
not earth.
But on the fourth morning
their heat glows
at the petals' very edge in a
burst
of gold
that explodes
around a centre now drained pale.

In my blue kitchen I found them;
a dozen stars gone
supernova
bursting
into a shrivelling morning
cold as space.

July 16

My husband killed our carpenter ants
this morning. He entered the attic
gliding snakelike through the passage
in the nursery closet. I handed after him
his light, three cans of ant poison
a mask against poisoning himself.
All morning I heard him, antlike
scratching at the insulation
tapping out white powder
in a deathly morse code.

He descended a grey-furred monster
covered with sweat and loose insulation
and with a childlike disappointment
that he did not see them die:
They are eating our house he said.

But he stayed to watch their frenzied arc
like poisoned shooting stars that rise
along the harsh dark rafters.

September 7

Against the moon
white plate
a tomato
rotted.
One soft green spot of mould
growing at the stem end
blossomed
turning half the tomato
soft brown red.
Clear rotten juice
moved over the moon
plate in runnels.
Seeds eased
out of the splitting
skin
in rich and fecund spoilage—
seeds for hybrid blooms
that never fruit—
or I would have left them to grow
in the dust that gathered
and in their own rot.

Augury
October, 1985

Mark off the templum
watch south.
And the birds—do they ascend
from left or from right
from instinct or from reason?
Do their flights bode well or ill?
Do they sing or spiral silently down?

I have seen them stop
the street to feed
on dropped grain,
careless in their hunger
to store seed.

Confused by wind,
flocks have flown north
feared the sky   flown low
till dizziness and time
crushed them in early storms.

Fledglings sleep in the grass
waiting for cats.
Younger than winter,
still they dread
what they should not know.

What does it augur,
this storm   these flights of birds?
Their hunger sings
through the drawn square of earth
where we watch descents,
listen to crushed silences,
and learn how to winter.

Flowers of Evil
October 29

A new translation of *Fleurs du Mal*
came by mail.
Malignant buds of styrofoam
cling to the vinyl cover
and grow off the pages.

In the garden
heads of sunflowers bow east
on hollow necks;
frost-killed petals form
the brown halo of an old painting.
The sunken heads are leprous
with seeds and brown-shelled pests.

You tell of such flowers grown in your dreams:
seeds burst to prickly bud in your mouth,
and when the pain had fully bloomed
you harvested slippery-thick stems
that slid like nausea from their rootspace
between sickened breaths.
You asked what they were.
Now I know you have eaten seeds
from the flowers of evil.

Pomegranate
November 11

Winter's first snowy day.
I peeled a pomegranate
standing exiled at the window
watching white blossoms
grow on the screen.

The leathery skin of the berry
protects intimate, mysterious chambers
whose shapes I can never predict.
So my thumb gouged the fruit;
splashes of red juice spread
on the window in relief
against the snow that clung
to the other side.

Persephone. You ate
three red seeds your first winter
in the underworld. Do you remember
their beautiful red bitterness,
the hard seed
centred
in a liquid gem?
What intimate chambers were gouged,
what blood spurted into winter
as you peeled your pomegranate?

Snow for a Drought

for Berhane Semere

This snow seems something from a child's
confectionery dreams—like feathers of spun sugar
heaped sweetly for us to glut our eyes.
I cannot wait to go in sober celebration
and clear my walk: under cover
of purpose I imagine I can toss it back
to the skies   if I wish.
In the tumuli
on bird feeder and fence post
light newly made blooms from flakes
like stars that shoot and glaze fires
in my own cold world.

As I clear my way
through garden, piling snow that will melt
to next year's lettuce, I think
a miracle would be such snow that falls
on the drought of soldiers burning fields
already burnt by the sun.

Snow on this drought, this death,
those tiny stars exploding cold
through fires that burn fields,
flakes that freeze hunger, then grow and bloom
like love with light that cools
and seeds the hopeful furrows
someone made in faith last year.

The Metaphysics of Divorce

How simple lives need no sense of humour
1972; 1984

Once because we believed it there
we could walk an invisible
sheltered edge
between windflung clots of snow
and rough red brick of Tudor dorms

Innocent of Catch-22's, we thought
nervous laughter at severed bodies
mocked the patterns we read
in dormitory windows:
lighted book-spread studies
and early darkened windows of lovers
we believed of use to chart our lives

You read Pooh's Tao
while some vision caught in my throat
between cords that laughed with sobbing
rehearsed Yosarian as he bandaged
his comrade's legs
and turned him over lovingly to watch
his guts fall out

Unsheltered now
by old buildings of youth
by simple patterns of study light and dark love
we walk enlightened home through different storms
knowing no asylum
Ours is no war only
small tussles with some Catch-22
that sever us from ourselves
each other

So we make jokes   They are not
particularly funny—only some proof
that we can play
at least
with language
with private history
while others seem
to play with lives

Each joke we make—banal or silly
vicious or good-natured—is a bandage
for your wounds   But through slow weeping
of my own I have come to know
that first aid is inadequate   that when
I turn you toward me to bless you
kiss you
I will finally see that your heart
is falling out

Family Portrait

In the mottled darkness, flashbulbs expose
two half-smiles. My child grins
but I do not fancy leering
for the next twelve months
from the top of my in-laws' TV.
And I do not know any more
how he wishes to cast himself
from the present
toward a frozen future.

The photographer knows every pattern
a family of three makes
on his rotating stools:
how we should turn or stand
how we should focus
on the negative's future.
We make a compact group, fit together snugly:
no technician knows patterns
the heart has not made of loving;
hands are not placed in poses
where they were not placed in love.

Yet my uneasiness will not smile.

On the mottled walls hang portraits
of cooing babies, chummy couples,
families on the beach with their dogs.
These photographs are smiling death masks
of wanderers who cannot turn back
through age, death,
loss of love, or growth
to time's smiling betrayal
of the negative.

Separation

Two weeks before he left
he filled the kindling box
with pieces of painted lumber.
As I watched my fire I wondered
what I burned—
house or life—
who built it, tore it down.

Later, wheeling his suitcase through the kitchen
he knocked from my daughter's shelf
three small pie tins she used for play.
On the linoleum, they winked bright and false
like hollow silver suns
in a dun sky.

I never guessed his going.
But, unheard, the house told me:
the meagre food,
the strange kindling, the broken,
empty thing.

Baba Doll

The broken Baba doll has fractures,
splinters all along the fringe
of her homely old shawl:
you might as well have dropped her
from twenty storeys
as from thirteen years.

Inside you will not find a perfect replica,
merely smaller, diminished by your departure,
but still whole and shapely.

Inside there are wicked fragments
caught in the yarn left from her knitting:
bent staples that will not bite
through the legal papers,
a patch she'd put on your leather jacket,
the sales receipt from the bear she bought you
that now, you tell her,
helps you recognize your girlfriend's apartment,
leftover love that will not fit in the deep-freeze.

Now that it's broken,
what does a doll do with all this stuff
that spills and trails around the house?

Captive Figure

Waiting in line
I unzip my daughter's snowsuit hood
to tease the child out of boredom
and out pours laughter:
I watch through a small absence
and can hear myself giddy, patient.
One arm, one eye have stretched beyond
the stone of loss, can stroke and tease my daughter,
can glimpse through a thin stone veil
my own bound delight.

Which is finished? The outstretched hand,
the finely carved, clear eye that sees
a need for laughter and strokes it into being?
Or the blind block of stone,
all its tangled ganglion turned inward?
Mute and solid, it insists
there is no captive figure inside
that might outstretch unfinished bounds.

A terrifying balance in the answer:
the outward laughter, the inner stone
are poised, divorced.
I cannot bend the uncarved hand
beyond this severed time
to wipe the stony lens from inturned eyes.

Pulling Taffy

I pulled taffy twice as a child:
my sister and I stretching the sweet strands,
folding them back on one another,
twisting
then stretching again until the sweetness
snapped with a promising crackle.

After you'd been gone a year
I hoped the sweet adolescent bond
that went back to a parked Oldsmobile,
the smell of starch in your shirt collars,
the tingle of crew cut under my fingers
would have pulled like taffy
to the snapping point.

Instead, our bond folds like history
repeating itself,
twisting around every act of my past
that brought me to the present,
forming a gnarled thread
that will not harden enough—
and turn to convenient hate—
to be dusted, wrapped, stored,
then found,
after a year's calm forgetting,
inedible.

In This Wind

In this wind
my poppies last two days
before the petals' sheer skin edge
is torn to the fleshy black base.
For two days springing clots of red
sway over my garden's purple sage
and dry green thyme.

The siberian elm,
not flexuous,
not in seedy bloom,
litters the lawn with brittle twigs
in the first day of wind:
deadwood, I say, hopefully.

In this wind
I dream nightly of abortions.
The tatter of falling branches awakens me
to remember some stranger I once loved
delivering abortions:
bringing down hospital hallways, grey streets, green paths
some parcel of my love for him that he has wrapped
in legal paper or in words
and I hold it once more, fondle my loves for him
until, stiff, white-gowned, he takes them from me.

In this wind
I abort and abort and abort
my love for him:
my deadwood love clots and litters
the hallways, streets, paths
while the pods of poppy seed
dance and rattle.

Braille Song

"Green pleasure or grey grief"
—Swinburne

I

Grief dictated a new language
to record my pleasure
in cats, tea, crickets,
in the changes of the moon
and the permanence of her revolutions;
to record my promise to myself
that upon my bed last Thursday
there was a cat curled, purring,
and that I had the power to carve
in the shape of her stroked fur
the shape of a moment's peace.
Or that blue deafness could not drown
crickets singing summer heat.
That I saw clearly
    Tuesday's moon a sharp disk of ice,
    Wednesday's a creature face shrouded in azure
when Monday time had stopped on a grating note
that played all week and sprinkled metal filings
on everything I saw.

II

Grief freezes eyes open,
pronounces the curse to stare unsleeping
on the lost world.
The once-ordinary-now-forbidden
is sentenced to be ever in view
through absence and change:
empty hangers, unused tea mug, silent meal.

My eyes ache, fighting their fix on the past,
but my fingers sing on the page
of a new language:
The crumble of earth, the texture of leaves
shape a braille that rises
surprising
from a grief that flattens the world
to its ancient limits.

III

Three a.m. My daughter's weeping
is muffled by dark blankets of sleep and fear.
Having had a nightmare she wants me
to bring back sleep.
(I have not been sleeping.
Parental irony: we give
our children what we cannot give ourselves.)

Rubbing her back I feel beneath the flannel
the lithe tenacity of childhood
summed in that muscle and bone.
Her decisive back belies
the softness of the sleep she seeks,
the mother comfort of my stroking,
my liquid songs.
A similarly sleepless cat comes,
settles on my settled hand,
adding her fur to the texture of soft sleep, hard bone.
Her rough purr counterpoints the flow of song.

My hand, between cat and child,
reads suddenly the unexpected braille
of purr and song,
of bone and fur:
the unmeasured textures of a single moment.

And the world becomes as round
as the raised dots of pleasure
that come through the hand,
to circumvent the griefblind, frozen
eye.

The Metaphysics of Divorce

I

Late sixties:
Dormitory weekends: rum and coke,
philosophical talk going ribald toward morning
as the sand candles guttered;
maybe some grass,
a towel stuffed under the door
to save others decisions of conscience.

We pursued labyrinthine conversations
of literature and philosophy
(and sex)   (listening to Beethoven),
politics and history
(and guys)   (Simon and Garfunkle),
some paths so goofy we'd trace them
back to origins
through the switchbacks of association,
fuelled by an odd compulsion
to name and place the conversational corners.

II

Late eighties: what conversations with my life—
string of associations, switchbacks—
lead to this moment
of late summer evening in my garden.
The scent of nicotiana blazes whitely through night air;
I walk among vegetables and roses, drinking scotch.
My child (her time with me half gone)
sleeps inside with cats.

Perplexed, I wonder what string of cause
connects the cars into their rhythm
on the main road, half a block away.
My spider web of thought follows them
through this northern city I'd never heard of
when, in another country, we talked of Hegel or Eliot.
(Besides, that wench is dead.)
Do they know the sound of their tires
intertwines with this skein of evening,
that someone asks questions, contemplates the cause
that intersects the sound of tires
and the smell of nicotiana?

III

The metaphysics of divorce:
so cut loose in time and space,
a lapse from believed past
and planned future.
A severing of bodies leads one to pose
odd questions about cause.

So I try to think of something determinant.
My mother, pregnant, tenderly, nervously
carrying the determinacy of genes
beneath a print cotton housedress.
Perhaps there it is also late summer;
she is barely showing
walking through her garden of chrysanthemums and phlox.
She might have predicted this poem,
my blue eyes, my ability at math.
But a pregnant woman seldom predicts grief,
which—though not genetic—is human.
She would not have seen the determinacy I now feel
about my own sleeping child,
seeing beyond her child to mine,
or the one, two years older, who never woke or slept.
Or the labyrinthine conversation of marriage,
carried on for thirteen years to disappear
in three days' time, no cause espoused.

If life's a conversation, then like talk
it too is full of clichés and surprised songs,
other speakers that interrupt and digress,
leading you from destinations
once inevitable.
But this metaphor is too indeterminate
tonight: it captures my surprise but fails
to entail the inevitability that I should be
drinking scotch, smelling nicotiana, that surely
in half an hour, when the night is too cold for bare arms
I will go in, smooth my daughter's hair away
from her sleeping face,
hold an old cat, begin to close some windows.

Disconnected as it is from philosophy,
from sand castles, from my wedding night,
this moment's potence—
the smell of damp earth mingling
with the zing of scotch along my tongue and brain,
the believed sound of sleeping child-breath,
questions of car tires that travel causal paths—
is its own perfect determinacy.

A Note on Dates

The oldest poems in this collection are those in the segment entitled "Journals of an Urban Gardener," with the exception of "Augury" (1985) and "Snow for a Drought," which was written during the first public awareness of the rebellion of Eritrea. The urban garden, with all its paradoxes and problems, is clearly central to my poetic cosmology; writing these poems made that centrality clear to me. Originally, these were "minor" lyrics written while I worked in the *Sturm und Drang* mode of Eliot and Pound's modernism, the poetics I seemed to explore endlessly as a graduate student. I have since thrown away the "sturm und drang" poems, while the pleasures and helpless struggles reflected in my microcosm have seemed to remain authentic in the context of a life that changes constantly.

A number of the poems in this collection benefitted directly from the editing skills of Patrick Friesen, notably "Death Songs for My Daughter" and some of the poems in "Journals of an Urban Gardener." During my apprenticeship with him in the Manitoba Writers' Guild Mentor Program in the fall of 1985, I wrote "Icarus," sections 2 and 3 of "Dumb Animals," "Augury," "Family Portrait," "Separation" and "In This Wind." While I am responsible for any poetic failings in these poems, Patrick can be credited with creating the rich and inviting atmosphere in which these poems were produced.

The most recent poems in the collection (written during 1988) include sections 1 and 4 of "Dumb Animals," "Humansong," "Braille Song" and "Metaphysics of Divorce." They reflect, I think, a typical postmodern anxiety about language and meaning.

Notes

"Humansong," page 5

The beginning of a fugue is constructed of a subject, which is a fairly brief and striking musical statement, and its answer, which is often presented in the dominant key.

"Cosmogony," page 11

A failed version of this poem was begun in the fall of 1978, after a stay in Neepawa, Manitoba, where I first met Diane Whitehouse; we were both teaching at the Family Art Camp. Diane's exhibit of *Rooms and Journeys* in 1986 at Gallery 1.1.1. finally provided a painterly image for the way in which the clichéd anonymity of hotel rooms provides its inhabitants with metaphorical canvases. When *Contemporary Verse* 2 published this poem in the summer of 1987 (Vol. 10, No. 4), one of Diane Whitehouse's paintings, *The Pool* (acrylic/oil) appeared on the cover.

The best-known painting of Norwegian expressionist Edvard Munch (1863-1944) is probably *The Scream*. Robert Hughes describes him as "the first modern painter to make a continuous study of the idea that personality is created by conflict" (*Shock of the New* [New York: Knopf, 1981], 276). The painting described in "Cosmogony" was part of a travelling exhibition of European art that visited the Winnipeg Art Gallery. Unlike conscientious, acquisitive gallery-goers, I do not recall its name, but I believe I have described it with fair accuracy.

"Dumb Animals: 4," page 26

The statement by Lacan is quoted from Luce Irigaray in her *This sex which is not one* (trans. Catherine Porter with Carolyn Burke [Ithaca: Cornell University Press, 1985], 88). Irigaray is quoting from Jacques Lacan in *Encore* XX (Paris, 1975). Lacan goes on to say, "Every reality is based upon and defined by a discourse."

"Descent of Inanna," page 31

For my introduction to the Sumerian myth of Inanna, I am indebted to Sylvia Brinton Perera's book, *Descent to the Goddess: A Way of Initiation for Women* (Toronto: Inner City Books, 1981). While there are many myths that explore an individual's descent to a god or goddess (see Campbell's *Hero of a Thousand Faces*, for example), the myth of Inanna is one of the oldest; the record that comes down to us on clay tablets is dated from the third millenium, B.C.

One advantage of employing mythical meta-narratives is that in spite of the spiritual and psychological resonances which they retain, they come to us in a form that is free from dogma. The writer can also, as Hawthorne knew, make of them what one wants or needs. I have, consequently, freely adapted to my needs the skeletal elements of "Inanna's descent."

Inanna was the Sumerian queen of heaven and earth; nevertheless she chose to descend to Ereshkigal's underworld, ostensibly to witness the funeral of Gugalanna, Ereshkigal's mate. The ruler of the underworld, who in some interesting ways is Inanna's dark mirror, is not pleased by Inanna's presence and instructs the gatekeeper to bring her "naked and bowed low" (Perera 9). Consequently, he removes an item of Inanna's clothing at each of the seven gates (though in the myth he does not give her a head of wheat in return). Subsequently, Ereshkigal kills Inanna; her corpse is hung on a meat hook, where it rots. Inanna has not entered the underworld with complete naïveté, however, but has instructed Ninshubur, her assistant, to effect her rescue if she does not return within three days. Ninshubur receives help from Enki, "god of waters and wisdom" (Perera 10), who fashions two small mourners from clay. They slip into the underworld and, by sympathizing with Ereshkigal, convince her to give them Inanna's corpse.

"Augury," page 44

Messages from the gods, in ancient Roman times, were sought before any important undertaking. An augur "marked off a *templum*, a rectangular space." After offering a prayer, "he sat looking southward. . . . Signs on the E. side (the augur's left) were regarded as propitious, on the W. as unfavourable." Omens might appear in the form of flights of birds, or other natural manifestations. (Sir Paul Harvey, *The Oxford Companion to Classical Literature* [Oxford: Oxford University Press, 1969], 65).

"How simple lives need no sense of humour," page 51

The catch-22 in Joseph Heller's book by the same name refers to an insoluble difficulty. One could get out of the military by claiming insanity, but recognition of one's insanity is regarded as a sane act. Yosarian, Heller's protagonist, attempts in the film to bandage a comrade's minor leg wounds, only to find, when he turns the comrade toward him, that his guts are falling out. In his memory, Yosarian repeatedly replays this moment.

"Captive Figure," page 57

When I visited Italy in 1978, I was deeply moved by Michaelangelo's *Captive Figures*, statues that are apparently unfinished, and that show the planned figure emerging from the stone. The figures, unfinished or not, appear to be struggling to rise out of their stony prisons. I was also fascinated with the controversy which has surrounded them as to whether they are finished or discarded works. Regardless of Michaelangelo's *intentions* (a dirty word in litcrit), they seemed to me to stand as works of art, to express an aesthetic and human struggle with metamorphosis.

"Braille Song," page 61

The source of the Swinburne quotation is "A Match" in *The Works of Charles Algernon Swinburne: Poems* (Philadelphia: David McKay, n.d.), 48-9.

"The Metaphysics of Divorce," page 64

There's a bit of literary in-breeding going on here. "But that was in another country / And besides, the wench is dead" comes from Marlowe's *The Jew of Malta*; Eliot uses those lines in his epigraph to "Portrait of a Lady."